W9-CCP-585

Earth

ELAINE LANDAU

Children's Press®
A Division of Scholastic Inc.
New York   Toronto   London   Auckland   Sydney
Mexico City   New Delhi   Hong Kong
Danbury, Connecticut

Content Consultant

Michelle Yehling

Astronomy Education Consultant

Aurora, Illinois

Reading Consultant

Linda Cornwell

Literacy Consultant

Carmel, Indiana

Library of Congress Cataloging-in-Publication Data

Landau, Elaine.
 Earth / by Elaine Landau.
   p. cm.—(A true book)
 Includes bibliographical references and index.
 ISBN-13: 978-0-531-12558-8 (lib. bdg.)   978-0-531-14788-7 (pbk.)
 ISBN-10: 0-531-12558-0 (lib. bdg.)   0-531-14788-6 (pbk.)
 1. Earth—Juvenile literature. I. Title. II. Series.
 QB631.4.L36 2007
 525—dc22   2007012278

All rights reserved. Published in 2008 by Children's Press, an imprint of Scholastic Inc.
Published simultaneously in Canada. Printed in the United States of America.
SCHOLASTIC, CHILDREN'S PRESS, A TRUE BOOK, and associated logos are trademarks
and/or registered trademarks of Scholastic Inc.
1 2 3 4 5 6 7 8 9 10 R 17 16 15 14 13 12 11 10 09

Find the Truth!

Everything you are about to read is true *except* for one of the sentences on this page.

Which one is **TRUE**?

T or F   Earth is the second-biggest planet in the solar system.

T or F   The same side of the moon always faces Earth.

Find the answer in this book.

Contents

THE **BIG** TRUTH!

Global Warming: What Can You Do?

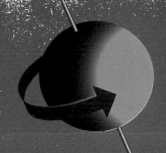

Earth spins like a top as it moves around the sun.

**You can see the moon high
above Earth's clouds.**

This image of Earth was created on a computer from data that a satellite collected. The satellite sent the data to computers on Earth, which made this picture.

CHAPTER 1

Planet Earth: Home Sweet Home

 Earth is sometimes called the Big, Blue Marble.

You can't see much of Earth when you are standing on it. Imagine, though, that you could fly above Earth in a spaceship. You would see that Earth is a big round ball like other planets in the **solar system**. The solar system is made up of the sun and all the objects that travel around it. Earth is the only planet that's just right for people and other life forms to survive.

This photo of the east coast of the United States was taken by a camera on a satellite. You can see white clouds over the Atlantic Ocean.

Earth looks blue because most of its surface is covered by water. Green and brown land rises above the water. Even from a spaceship, you might see signs of life on Earth. For example, you could see glowing lights from big cities at night.

Earth is different from other planets in many ways. For one thing, so far Earth is the only planet on which scientists have found life. What makes Earth so special? Let's take a closer look at our planet.

Just Like Home?

On April 24, 2007, Swiss **astronomers** found a planet where they thought life might exist. Gliese (GLEE-zuh) 581 c **orbits**, or travels around, a red star about 20.5 light years (120 trillion miles; 193 trillion kilometers) from Earth.

Later in 2007, astronomers found evidence that this planet was too hot to support life. Another planet in the same solar system seemed promising, however. Gliese 581 d is likely to have water, an **atmosphere**, and temperatures suitable for life.

Are there aliens on Gliese 581 d? Astronomers need more information to know for sure!

It would take 20.5 years for radio waves from Earth to reach Gliese 581 c.

This is an artist's drawing of Gliese 581 c and the star that it orbits.

This illustration shows Earth and part of the sun. On average, the sun is about 93 million miles (150 million km) from Earth. In reality, Earth would look much smaller.

CHAPTER 2

Earth's Journey

Earth travels in its orbit at 66,700 miles per hour.

Earth is one of eight planets in our solar system. The others are Mercury, Venus, Mars, Jupiter, Saturn, Uranus, and Neptune. The sun is at the center of the solar system. Planets and other space objects orbit the sun. At least 162 moons travel around the eight planets.

Comets are icy objects that orbit the sun.

All About Orbit

The planets orbit the sun. Planets orbit in a flattened circle called an ellipse (ee-LIPS).

What keeps the planets from flying out into space? The sun's **gravity** pulls on the planets and holds them in orbit. Gravity is the force that pulls objects toward each other.

You could jump higher on a planet with weaker gravity.

Earth's Place in the Universe

A.D. 150

Ptolemy (TOL-uh-mee)
This Greek thinker says the sun and other planets circle Earth. People believe this for 1,000 years.

All objects have some gravity. Massive objects such as the sun have strong gravity. Earth has weaker gravity than the sun. Earth's gravity is strong enough to hold you down on the planet, though. It is also strong enough to hold on to the moon that orbits Earth.

1540s
Copernicus (kuh-PUR-nih-kuhss)
This Polish astronomer discovers that the sun is at the center of the solar system. The new idea makes some people angry, but he is right!

1925
Edwin Hubble
This American astronomer helps us see how huge the universe is. He finds that certain objects in the night sky are actually distant galaxies, or collections of millions or billions of stars.

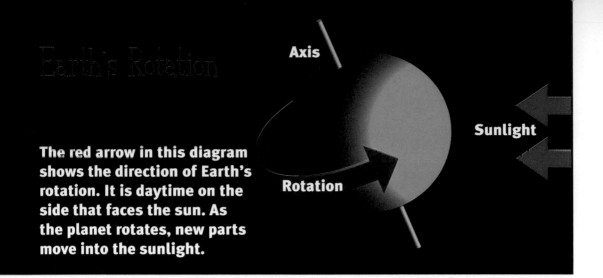

Earth's Rotation

Axis

Sunlight

Rotation

The red arrow in this diagram shows the direction of Earth's rotation. It is daytime on the side that faces the sun. As the planet rotates, new parts move into the sunlight.

Years and Days

The time it takes a planet to orbit the sun once equals one year. It takes Earth about 365 days to orbit the sun. So one year equals about 365 days.

As a planet orbits the sun, it also spins on its **axis**. An axis is an imaginary line running from north to south through the center of a planet or a moon.

The amount of time it takes a planet to spin around once on its axis equals one day on that planet. It takes Earth 23 hours and 56 minutes to complete one spin. So we say a day is 24 hours long.

How Big Is Earth?

Earth's **diameter** is 7,926 miles (12,756 km). Does this make Earth a big planet? Not really.

Jupiter, Saturn, Uranus, and Neptune are much larger than Earth. They are called the gas giants— huge planets made mostly of liquid and gas.

But Earth's closest neighbors make our planet look big. Mars, Mercury, and Venus are all rocky planets like Earth. But they are all smaller than Earth.

Jupiter is the largest planet in the solar system.

Mercury Venus Earth Mars Jupiter Saturn Uranus Neptune

Pluto (dwarf planet)

Uranus

Jupiter

Mars

Mercury

asteroid belt

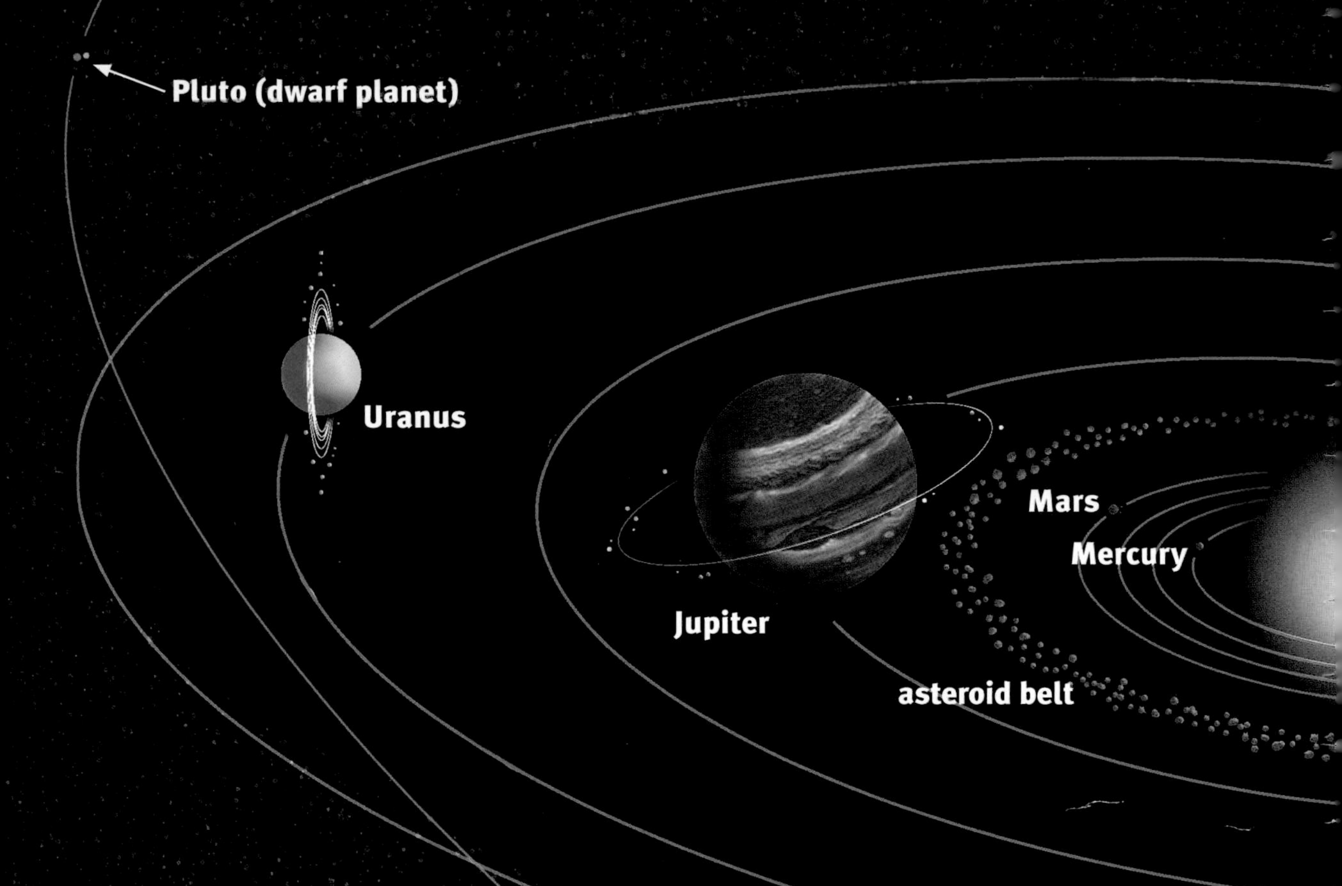

Earth

- Third planet from the sun
- Fifth-largest planet
- Diameter: 7,926 mi.
  (12,756 km)
- Length of a day: 23 hours, 56 minutes
- Length of a year: About 365 days

Kuiper Belt

sun

Venus

Earth's moon

Earth

Saturn

Neptune

Life exists almost everywhere on Earth. This coral reef in the Pacific Ocean is made of thousands of tiny animals. Fish feed on plants and animals that live in the reef.

CHAPTER 3

Conditions for Life

Tiny creatures have been found as deep as 4 miles under Earth's surface.

Earth is different from its neighbors in space. Our planet is full of plants, animals, and other living things. Astronomers have studied the planets and many other space objects in Earth's solar system. They have found no proof of life anywhere but Earth.

Tiny organisms have existed on Earth for millions of years. This one-celled protist is seen through a microscope.

Water World

How can millions of life forms call Earth home? Special conditions on Earth make life possible. One of the most important is water. All living things on Earth need water to survive.

There is a lot of water on Earth. Earth's deep oceans cover about 70 percent of the planet's surface. Oceans are full of salt water, however. Most land animals and plants need freshwater, or water with no salt in it. That's the kind of water you drink.

Out of every 100 drops of water on Earth, only 3 drops are freshwater.

Most lakes and rivers are freshwater.

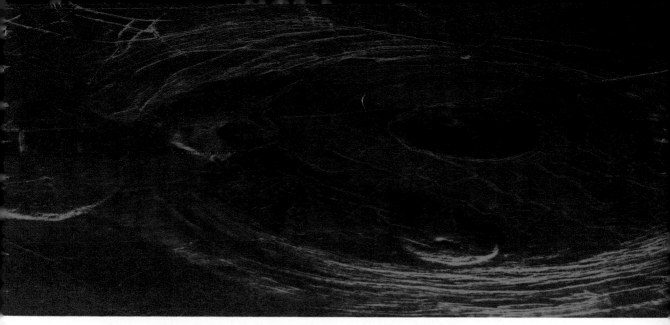

This image shows a crater, or hole, on Venus. Venus has a surface temperature that can reach almost 900°F (500°C).

Not Too Hot—Or Too Cold

Another important condition for life is Earth's distance from the sun. Mercury and Venus are closer to the sun than Earth is. On those planets, it is too hot for living creatures.

The gas giants are much farther away from the sun. Those planets do not get as much of the sun's warmth. Astronomers believe that these planets are too cold for living creatures to survive.

What a Gas!

The third important condition for life on Earth is the atmosphere. Earth's atmosphere contains gases called nitrogen, oxygen, and carbon dioxide. Most life on Earth needs oxygen to survive. Plants use carbon dioxide to make food.

The leaves of a sunflower plant use carbon dioxide and energy from the sun to make food.

Sunscreen

Earth's atmosphere acts like a sunscreen. It protects our planet from some of the sun's harmful rays. These rays could hurt plants and animals.

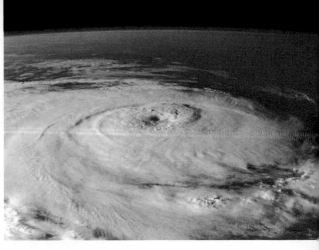

Earth's atmosphere is largely responsible for its weather. This view from space shows a hurricane on Earth.

Earth's atmosphere also soaks up heat from the sun. It keeps Earth from getting too hot during the day. And it holds on to some heat at night. So Earth doesn't get too cold for living things when the sun goes down.

Compare Earth to the moon, which has little atmosphere. During the day, the temperature of the moon's surface can be hot enough to boil water! At night, the moon's surface can cool to −387°F (−233°C).

Q. How we can help fight global warming?

A. Here are some changes you can make to put less carbon dioxide into the atmosphere:

• Ride your bike or walk instead of asking your parents to drive you somewhere.

• Use less energy. Turn off lights, the TV, and the computer when you are not using them.

• Open a window and switch off the air conditioner.

• Encourage adults to plant trees. Trees absorb carbon dioxide from the air.

• "Reduce, Reuse, Recycle." Making products uses energy. Throwing away products that could be reused is wasteful.

Smoke from factories can dump carbon dioxide and other chemicals into the air. Rising levels of carbon dioxide in the air may be increasing Earth's temperature.

Global Warming:
What Can You Do?

Q: What is global warming?

A: Earth is getting warmer. Weather patterns are changing. Some places are getting less rain. Other places are getting more rain. Ice at the North Pole and the South Pole seems to be melting faster than it is refreezing.

Q: What is causing global warming?

A: Most scientists think that extra carbon dioxide and other gases in the atmosphere are causing global warming.

Most of Earth's ancient rocks are buried under soil, but not all of them. In the Uinta Mountains in Utah, you can find traces of rocks that were formed more than 100 million years ago.

CHAPTER 4

What Is Earth Made Of?

Some rocks near Earth's surface are 4 billion years old.

We know that most of Earth's surface is covered by water. What is the rest of the planet made of? What is the structure of Earth? Here is your chance to take a look inside.

This is a fossil of a fern. A fossil is a trace of a plant or an animal from millions of years ago preserved as rock.

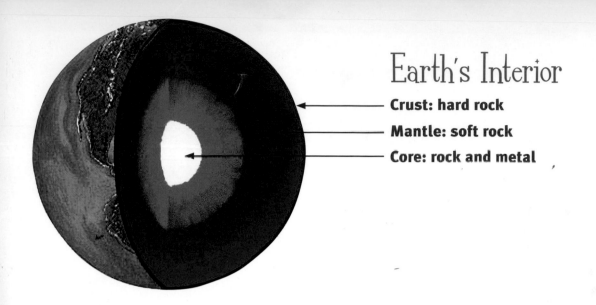

Earth's Interior

Crust: hard rock

Mantle: soft rock

Core: rock and metal

Three Layers

Think of Earth as a giant, hard-boiled egg. The rock and dirt that you see is just a thin layer. This thin layer is called the **crust**. It is like an egg's shell. Even the oceans have a layer of crust beneath them.

Under the crust is a thick layer of soft rock. The rock is soft because it's hot. This is called the mantle. The heat comes from Earth's deepest layer. In the middle of the planet is a round ball called the core. The temperature in the core might reach 11,000°F (6,000°C).

On the Surface

Earth is a **terrestrial** (tuh-RES-tree-uhl) planet. That means it has a hard, rocky surface. Terrestrial planets have mountains, valleys, and volcanoes. Many of Earth's volcanoes are still active. This means they can erupt, or shoot out, gas and **lava**.

A volcano called Kilauea (kih-luh-WAY-ah) erupts on the island of Hawaii.

Crater Lake in Oregon formed after a volcano collapsed 7,700 years ago. Water filled the huge hole it left behind.

Venus, Mars, and Mercury are also terrestrial planets. All four terrestrial planets have holes called impact craters in their surfaces. These craters were created when asteroids and other space objects crashed into the planets.

Most of Earth's craters can't easily be seen anymore. This is because wind and rain have worn them down.

Meteor Crater

Meteor Crater was made about 50,000 years ago. A giant space rock called a **meteorite** crashed into Earth. It smashed a big hole in the planet.

Meteor Crater is more than 4,000 feet (1,200 meters) wide. A 50-story building could stand up inside the hole and not reach the top.

In the past, astronauts went to Meteor Crater to train for trips to the moon.

Thousands of tourists travel to the Arizona desert every year to see Meteor Crater.

Moving Plates

You have already imagined Earth as an egg. Now think of it as a cracked egg. The crust that surrounds Earth is broken into large pieces. The different pieces are called plates. These plates slide slowly across each other.

You don't usually feel Earth's plates moving. This is because the movement happens very slowly. Plates move at about the same rate that your fingernails grow. Sometimes, however, people do feel the plates moving. Moving plates can cause earthquakes!

Each year, the Atlantic Ocean gets about 1 inch wider. The two plates that form it are moving away from each other. This is creating new rock in the middle.

Growing Mountains

The moving plates cause other, slower changes on Earth. Mountain ranges may grow when plates push against each other, for example. Plates pushing together cause rock to move upward. It takes millions of years to make a mountain this way.

Earth is an exciting place. Our planet is always changing. There is a lot going on beneath our feet.

In southern California, you can see part of the boundary where two of Earth's plates meet. This boundary is called the San Andreas Fault.

This computer graphic shows how the moon might look if you were floating high above Earth's clouds.

34

CHAPTER 5

Earth's One and Only Moon

More than 70 spacecraft have been sent to Earth's moon.

Earth's moon looks far away. But it's much closer than any other space object. Astronomers know more about our moon than about any other planet or moon. Earth's moon is still the only other place in the solar system that human beings have visited.

The moon's mountains and valleys look like light and dark spots from Earth.

The moon is about four times smaller than Earth. The moon also has less gravity than Earth. If you were walking on the moon, you would feel very light.

Here an astronaut from *Apollo 17* walks on the moon in 1972. Astronauts from six missions brought back 842 pounds (382 kilograms) of rock and soil from the moon.

The Moon's Path

The moon orbits Earth. It takes 29.5 days for the moon to circle Earth once. It takes the same amount of time for the moon to rotate on its axis.

Cameras on *Apollo 16* photographed the moon in 1972. On the right side of this image are parts of the "dark side" of the moon.

The identical rates of orbiting and rotating does something odd. The moon spins so the same side is always facing Earth. We see only one side of the moon. The side of the moon we can't see is often called the dark side of the moon. But it isn't really always dark there.

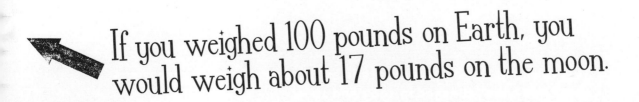

If you weighed 100 pounds on Earth, you would weigh about 17 pounds on the moon.

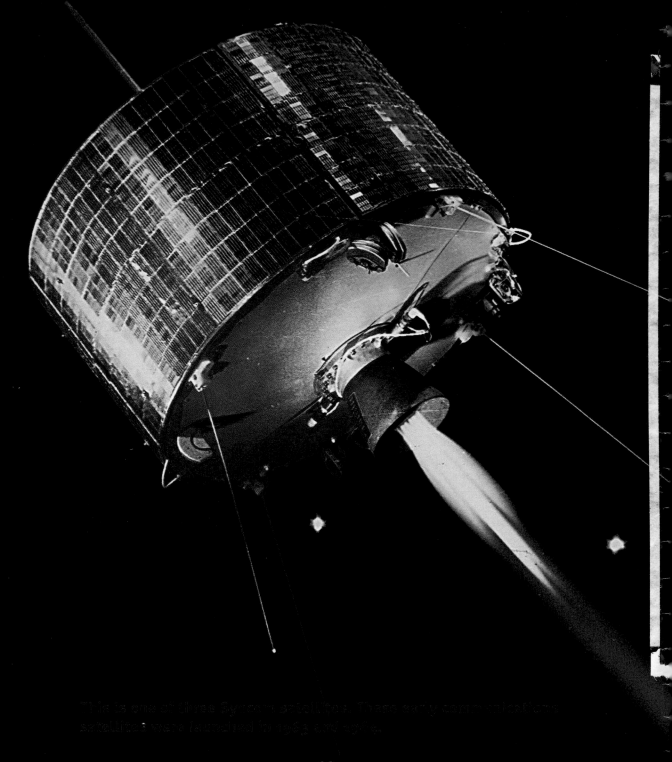

This is one of three Syncom satellites. These early communications satellites were launched in 1963 and 1964.

CHAPTER 6

Blast Off!
From Earth to Space

One of the satellites orbiting Earth is a space station where astronauts live.

Astronomers began sending **satellites** into space about 50 years ago. These satellites orbit Earth. Some have cameras to take pictures. Some carry instruments to study the planet and other space objects. Other satellites send signals to cell phones, radios, and TVs.

This illustration shows an artificial satellite orbiting Earth. About 3,000 of these satellites are now circling the planet.

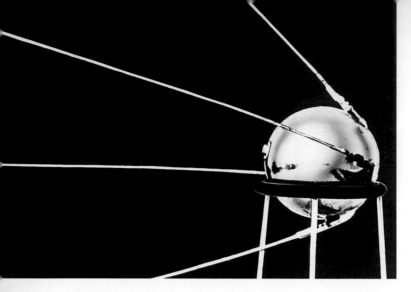

Sputnik I circled Earth about once every 98 minutes.

The First Satellites

The first man-made satellite to orbit Earth was named *Sputnik* (SPUHT-nik). The Soviet Union launched it on October 4, 1957. *Sputnik* was only 23 inches (58 centimeters) across and weighed about 184 pounds (83 kg).

American scientists quickly built and launched their own satellites in the late 1950s and early 1960s. These missions helped scientists learn how to launch objects into space. This helped them plan larger missions.

Moon Missions

The Apollo space program began in 1966. It sent astronauts to the moon to study it in person. Astronauts landed on the moon for the first time in 1969. Other astronauts made five more trips to the moon. The last one was in 1972.

Space stations have also been launched into orbit around Earth. Space stations are orbiting science laboratories. Astronauts live in the space stations to perform experiments and to gather information. They learn more about space and more about Earth.

Several astronauts have lived for more than a year aboard a space station.

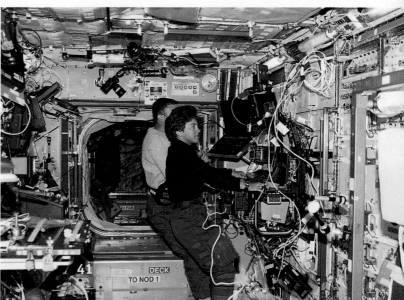

Astronomers continue to learn about our planet. They study it from space and from the ground. Still, there are many things astronomers don't know about Earth. Maybe someday they will discover new ways to learn about Earth. Perhaps you will be one of these astronomers! ★

Using high-powered telescopes, astronomers continue to learn more about the objects in the solar system.

True Statistics

Third planet from the sun

Classification: Terrestrial planet

Diameter: 7,926 mi. (12,756 km)

Main atmospheric gases: Nitrogen and oxygen

Approximate age: 4.5 to 4.6 billion years

Population: 6.6 billion

Highest temperature: 136°F (58°C)

Lowest temperature: −126°F (−88°C)

Distance from the sun: About 93 million mi. (150 million km)

Length of a day: 23 hours, 56 minutes

Length of a year: About 365 days

Distance to moon: 238,855 mi. (384,400 km)

Did you find the truth?

F Earth is the second-biggest planet in the solar system.

T The same side of the moon always faces Earth.

Resources

Books

Asimov, Isaac. *Earth*. Milwaukee, WI: Gareth Stevens, 2002.

Buckley, James. *Space Heroes: Amazing Astronauts*. New York: DK Publishing, 2004.

Hansen, Rosanna. *Mysteries in Space*. Danbury, CT: Children's Press, 2005.

Nault, Jennifer. *Earthquakes*. New York: Weigl, 2005.

Petersen, Christine. *Conservation*. Danbury, CT: Children's Press, 2004.

Taylor-Butler, Christine. *Earth*. Danbury, CT: Children's Press, 2008.

Van Rose, Susanna. *Earth*. New York: DK Publishing, 2005.

Webster, Christine. *Mountains*. Mankato, MN: Capstone Press, 2005.

Whitehouse, Patricia. *Earth*. Chicago: Heinemann Library, 2004.

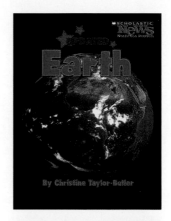

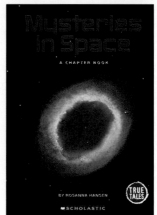

Organizations and Web Sites

Earth Observatory

www.earthobservatory.nasa.gov

Visit this Web site for interesting information about Earth.

National Space Society

www.nss.org

1620 I Street NW, Suite 615

Washington, DC 20006

202-429-1600

This organization works to help humans live and work in space.

Visible Earth

www.visibleearth.nasa.gov

Check out this site for great pictures of Earth from space.

Places to Visit

Kennedy Space Center

Kennedy Space Center, FL 32899

www.ksc.nasa.gov

Explore NASA's launch headquarters and learn more about some of the organization's space missions.

American Museum of Natural History

Central Park West at 79th Street

New York, NY 10024

212-769-5100

Find out what's lurking under Earth's rock, at the bottom of the oceans, and up in space.

Important Words

astronomers (uh-STRAW-nuh-murz) – scientists who study the planets, stars, and space

atmosphere (AT-mu-sfihr) – the blanket of gases that surrounds a planet or a moon

axis (AK-siss) – an imaginary line that runs through the center of a planet or other object

crust – the outermost layer of a rocky planet or moon

diameter (dye-A-muh-tur) – the distance across the center of a round object

gravity – a force that pulls two objects together

lava – hot melted rock, or melted rock that has cooled and hardened

meteorite (MEE-tee-uh-RITE) – a space object that has crashed into a planet

orbits – travels around an object such as a sun or planet

satellites – objects that orbit a space object

solar system (SOH-lur SISS-tuhm) – a sun and all the objects that travel around it

terrestrial (tuh-RES-tree-uhl) – the name for the four planets closest to the sun that have a surface of solid rock

Index

About the Author

Award-winning author Elaine Landau has a bachelor's degree from New York University and a master's degree in library and information science from Pratt Institute.

She has written more than 300 non-fiction books for children and young adults. Although Ms. Landau often writes on science topics, she especially likes writing about planets and space.

She lives in Miami, Florida, with her husband and son. The trio can often be spotted at the Miami Museum of Science and Space Transit Planetarium. You can visit Elaine Landau at her Web site: www.elainelandau.com.

PHOTOGRAPHS © 2008: Alamy Images/Natural History Museum: 27; Art Resource, NY/Victoria and Albert Museum, London: 12; Corbis Images: 40 (Bettmann), 13 (Stefano Bianchetti), 15 (Martin Kommesser/IAU), 26 (Scott T. Smith); Danita Delimont Stock Photography/Paul Thompson: 22; Dembinsky Photo Assoc.: 29 (Phil Degginger), 5 bottom, 34 (Phil Degginger/NASA), 41 (NASA); ESO Press Photo: 9; Getty Images: cover (Earth Imaging), 24 (Bruce Forster), 10 (Denis Scott), back cover (World Perspectives); Minden Pictures: 18 (Fred Bavendam), 20 (Yva Momatiuk/John Eastcott); NASA: 38 (GSFC), 36 (JSC), 3, 6 (Reto Stockli/Alan Nelson/Fritz Hasler); Nature Picture Library Ltd./Aflo: 23; Pat Rasch: 5 top, 14, 16, 17; Peter Arnold Inc./Kevin Schafer: 33; Photo Researchers, NY: 39 (Julian Baum), 42 (James King-Holmes), 37 (NASA), 8 (Orbimage), 21 (Detlev van Ravenswaay); Phototake: 19 (Dennis Kunkel), 11 (LookatSciences); Photri Inc./NASA: 28; Scholastic Library Publishing, Inc.: 44; Still Media/John Warden: 30; Superstock, Inc.: 35; The Image Works/Topham/Fortean: 31; VEER: 4.